Table of Contents

3 | **Summary**

8 | Chapter 1 - **The Significance of Public Speaking**

9 | How Public Speaking Has Changed the World
12 | The Role of Pubic Speaking in Career Development

16 | Chapter 2 - **Fear of Public Speaking**

17 | The Science Behind Your Fear of Public Speaking

22 | Chapter 3 - **Prepare**

39 | Chapter 4 - **Practice**

50 | Chapter 5 - **Present**

58 | Chapter 6 - **Finding Speaking Opportunities Through Different Media**

65 | Chapter 7 - **Conclusion**

Summary

Public speaking is consistently rated in surveys as one of people's greatest fears.

Modern science has traced the roots of this terror to the dawn of humankind, when rejection by our peers really was a matter of life and death. Understanding that this fear is something that everyone feels is the first step to overcoming it and starting to unlock the potential that inspirational public speaking has to change your career, your life, and your world.

In this book I show you how you too can use simple structures and tips to transform yourself from a nervous speaker into an influential orator. All you need to do is follow the stages of what I call "the 3 Ps of public speaking success" – prepare, practice, and present.

I discuss each of these in great detail with a wealth of practical tips to cover every step of the way on the journey from a fear of public speaking to talking like a TED superstar. I also draw on the work of great names in the field like Cicero, Abraham Lincoln, Martin Luther King, and Homer Simpson, to give you the tricks of the trade that will help you to overcome your own mind-made problems which are the only thing getting in the way of public speaking success.

Let's get started on that journey and remember, as one of history's most iconic speeches put it, "the only thing we have to fear is fear itself…" Introduction - Facing Up to America's Number One Fear…

"According to most studies, people's number one fear is public speaking. Number two is death. Death is number two. Does that sound right? This means to the average person, if you go to a funeral, you're better off in the casket than doing the eulogy." -Jerry Seinfeld

Any of the following sound familiar? You're about to take to the stage to deliver a major presentation in front of a crowd. Throughout the day you've been watching others speak, how natural, cool, calm, and collected they all seemed. But you're the exact opposite. While the event organizer is introducing you as an expert in your field, you're feeling like you'd rather by hiding away in a hole in the ground. Yours palms are sweaty, your face is red, and your throat's so dry that you fear that even if you face up to taking the stage no words will come out your mouth.

Sounds familiar? Maybe you've experienced something like that in reality, or in a nightmare. But if so, does it make you feel any better to know that numerous studies, from 1973's "Survey of American Fears" onwards, really have put fear of public speaking at or near the top of people's lists of things that terrify them?

Or might it reassure you to know that some of the world's greatest speakers have admitted to their own anxieties when called to the stage? Consider this from Mark Twain, the great American humorist of the 19th century, "there are two types of speakers: Those who get nervous and those who are liars."

Or is it any consolation to know that modern science reckons that fear of public speaking really is universal and has roots deep in our pre-history, when rejection by your peers actually was a matter of life and death?

Does any of that make you feel better about the prospect of public speaking? I really hope so because it is my intention in this book to help you to overcome that fear and show you how you can become a fantastic public speaker. And the first part of doing this is understanding both the roots and the universality of our fear - it is simply one of those things that make us human.

The next part of overcoming the fear comes from following the tips and tricks that I recommend under the headings of what I call the 3 Ps of Public Speaking - Prepare, Practice and Present. Although every great speech is different and there is no single formula for success, you can be sure that all great speakers follow the order of the 3 Ps and apply at least some of the big selection of the advice that I share with you here - advice that comes from both ancient experts in the art of public speaking and from the best of what modern science has to tell us about how to make speeches that have real impact on your audience.

But you may be asking, why bother with this anyway? Why should I face these fears and what does it matter to me to go through the struggle of becoming a great public speaker? Can't I just carry on as I am, keeping my head down, dodging presentations, and leaving them to those crazy colleagues who want to do them?

This question is answered in chapter one of the book - The Significance of Public Speaking which takes us on a whistle stop tour from pre-historic caves to TED Talks to explain, through inspiring examples, how great speeches have shaped the world we live in today. Then, moving from the global to the personal level, I demonstrate how important public speaking is for your personal development and career prospects. Starting with the story of how an opportunity to give a high-profile speech became the launching pad for one man's ascent to the world's top job. By the end of this chapter you'll understand exactly how public speaking can help your own career to take off and to stay high-flying.

The second chapter - Fear of Public Speaking - introduces in more detail the number one enemy that we need to overcome to achieve the benefits of great public speaking for ourselves - our own fear. Again we start by taking things back to pre-history, to understand what modern science can tell us about this ancient fear, so that through understanding we can learn to tame our fears and begin to turn them to our advantage.

Chapter three starts to get into the detail of how to start conquering your fear and by introducing the first of our 3 Ps of public speaking - Prepare. Here I show you how to prepare a winning speech, taking account of what ancient orators and modern scientists can teach us about structures and the rhetorical touches that win over your audience. I also look at the different purposes of public speaking - to entertain, educate, encourage change, entice, and eulogize - and explain how to take your overall aim into account when preparing a winning speech.

Chapter four - Practice - shows you the steps to take to turn a super presentation on paper into a superstar speech that flies in real life. From the tale of a TED talker who rehearsed 200 times, to a detailed analysis of how Martin Luther King's delivery helped his dream resonate around the world, this chapter shows you how practice really does make perfect. By the end of it you'll understand why some authorities say that 90% of how well your presentation goes is due to what you do you take the stage and learn how your own steps in rehearsal can set you up for success.

Chapter five - Present - takes us right back to where this introduction started, at the moment when you're about to take the stage. It takes you through the last-minute preparations that will help you keep your cool in the heat of the moment and shows you how to deal with any unexpected surprises that real-life presenting can throw at you.

After you've digested all of that you'll be raring to go and take on the world by getting some speaking engagements booked. Chapter six - Finding Speaking Opportunities Through Different Media - shows you just how to do that, and introduces you to all the various media through which you make your voice heard and can get invaluable real-life practice in preparation for the high-stakes presentation events that will define your career.

Finally, chapter seven, the book's Conclusion, end things the way every good presentation should with a summation of all the key lessons and an inspiring message to send you on your way into the world of public speaking success.

Sounds good? Then let's go. First stop is a look at how public speaking has shaped our world, and could help to transform your life too...

Chapter 1

The Significance of Public Speaking

How Public Speaking Has Changed the World

Public speaking is one of the oldest and most important forms of human art.

Think about it - the ability to make those complicated strings of meaningful sounds that we call speech is one of the key characteristics that distinguishes us from the rest of the animal kingdom. We don't know exactly when homo sapiens learned to make those sounds. But we do know that using words to transfer complex ideas is an exclusively human thing. Some other animals communicate through noise for sure, but it is not very likely we will hear the gorilla "Gettysburg Address" anytime soon.

Speech doesn't just distinguish us from other animals, it was the primary force that drove our successful expansion over almost all the habitable spaces of the globe and has even enabled exploratory missions into space. How could any of this occurred without the power of speech, which enables the establishment of common bonds, the sharing of complex ideas, and the implementation of complex collaboration.

And how particularly important in all this is the ancient art of public speaking? Blessed as it is with the magical power to touch the hearts and change the minds of masses - inspiring collective action in ways that have time and again shaped and reshaped our world. Who knows what great historic speeches occurred back in the mists of pre-history? Speeches which inspired actions that continue to shape the world around us, even today.

We certainly know that by the time history started to be written down, the names of great public speakers were recorded and celebrated.

The details of great speeches have been passed down over thousands of years and their words can still inspire and change the world today. In chapter three we'll meet one of those great ancient orators, the Roman senator Cicero, and learn how a five-point plan he scribbled on parchment over two thousand years ago can help us when we're putting our PowerPoint slides together today.

The significance of public speaking two change the world is evident when we consider the impact of some of the greatest speeches of the last few centuries. Think about Abraham Lincoln's "Gettysburg Address" which, in just 272 words, redefined what it means to be American and which was, according to Senator Charles Sumner, more significant than the battle it commemorated. Or Dr Martin Luther King's "I Have a Dream Speech" which remains perhaps the most significant moment of the whole civil rights struggle, and an ongoing inspiration to people struggling for freedom worldwide.

Even now in our digital age, which has revolutionized so much about the ways in which we communicate, the art of public speaking is still highly valued. The enormous popularity of 'TED Talks' attests to the fact that old fashioned oratory remains as popular as ever. In our modern era of information onslaught, we are even more grateful for great speakers who can distill the most important information that we need to know and can present it in ways which inspires people to change themselves and the world in positive ways.

To sum up, humans are blessed with the potential to speak eloquently, to fire the imagination of our listeners and to inspire them to do great, or terrible, things. This power receives its greatest expression in public speaking. As always with great power comes great responsibility. The skills of public speaking, when used well and responsibly, have great potential to help us progress and to make the world a better place.

Now you might be thinking - this is all well and good but what's it got to do with me? The answer is, even if you're not aiming to change the world, a heck of a lot. Public speaking, as we shall see, is an increasingly essential skill that enables you to improve your life, develop professionally, and to progress in your career.

Let's start, for some inspiration, by looking at one speech from recent years which put the speaker on the path to the world's top job. Then we'll drill down into the advantages that public speaking prowess can give you as you look to advance your own career - in terms of improving your performance, enhancing your image, and giving you essential exposure.

The Role of Public Speaking in Career Development

Performance - excelling in public speaking situations requires the development of skills and attributes that are highly desirable to employers.

The Democratic Party Convention in Boston, Massachusetts in July 2004, a virtually unknown young Illinois state senator took to the stage to give a keynote speech. He introduced himself to the convention, and to the world, as "a skinny kid with a funny name". But when he left the stage to a standing ovation just under twenty minutes later that name was reverberating around the world.

Shortly after the speech MSNBC's Chris Matthews predicted, "I have seen the first black president there." And just over four years later Matthews was proved right, as Barack Obama ascended to the top job in the world. A more striking recent example of the importance of public speaking for career development could hardly be found.

But ex-President Obama is far from the only recent example of someone who made a speech that made their career. Steve Jobs was, of course, already famous as the founder of Apple, but it was his legendary presentations of new products that cemented his iconic status around the world. While the TED Talks series have helped to catapult many academics, who were once merely known in their fields, into international fame with numbers of YouTube hits that rival some pop stars.

You might not be pursuing the presidency of the United States or aspiring to worldwide fame, but it is still likely that public speaking prowess will be one of the essential elements of the skill set required to achieve your career goals. A widely quoted 2012 study found that 70% of all jobs involve public speaking, and of course that figure increases the more senior the level of the job.

While a Prezi survey quoted in Forbes magazine also found that 70% of Americans who give presentations as part of their jobs think public speaking skills are critical to their success in their role (the article's author's response to this? "The other 30% don't know it yet.")

Author and management consultant Harvey Coleman claimed, in his classic 1996 book "Empowering Yourself", that the three key ingredients of a successful career are performance, image and exposure (or PIE). But what order of importance do you think he put the three in? Actually, the exact opposite to the way you might imagine - with exposure (responsible, according to Coleman, for 60% of your success) first, image (30%) second, and performance (10%) third.

On one level it's an astonishing conclusion, but it should come as no surprise to all those people toiling away and doing great jobs but never making progress in their career. They are probably assuming hard work and quality is enough, while neglecting their image and not getting themselves enough exposure.

The great news is that public speaking can help your career in terms of all the three pieces of the PIE - performance, image, and exposure - let's see how.

Performance - excelling in public speaking situations requires the development of skills and attributes that are highly desirable to employers. A 2014 survey quoted by the BBC showed that "oral communication" is the number one skill that recruiters look for, with "presentation skills" rated number four.

Beyond that, well-developed and delivered speeches require the acquisition and employment of skills that can improve your performance in a wide range of work situations, including critical thinking, structuring arguments convincingly and communicating clearly. The confidence that comes from overcoming your fears and becoming an excellent speaker is also an invaluable attribute in terms of improving your performance, especially as you have to face the challenges of more senior roles.

Image - Having a good image increases your chance of delivering a well-received presentation and giving a well-received presentation improves your image. It's a lovely virtuous circle if you can get yourself inside of it. Stepping up and delivering a great presentation sets you aside from your colleagues, especially in a context where many colleagues will try anything to avoid presenting duties (a 2014 survey conducted by Harris Poll showed that 20% would pass responsibility to a colleague if asked to give a presentation, even if it meant them losing respect in work).

Delivering a great speech communicates exactly the image of yourself that you want to get ahead in work - professional, poised, confident, and equipped with the skill set needed to impress clients and senior colleagues.

Exposure - giving presentations is a great way to get noticed, both by prospective employers and by senior management in your own company. A 2013 IBM report targeted at female managers aiming to become executives recommended signing up for speaking engagements as a keyway to raise your profile. Conference speaking also provides great opportunities for networking, both with your fellow speakers and with the audience members. Chapter six has lots more tips for how you can secure yourself speaking opportunities at conferences and all sorts of events to develop your skills, improve your image, and increase your exposure.

A specific aspect of exposure is through job interviews. Being well-known within your own company helps get you more interviews for promotions. Being well known in your field helps get you other opportunities at other companies too. The skills required for public speaking, such as the ability to concisely, clearly, and confidently communicate your message, are invaluable for any job interview situation. Plus, many job interviews nowadays, especially for top jobs, include a requirement to give a presentation as part of the process.

Hopefully by now the potential of public speaking skills to be a positive force in your life and career is fully apparent. Now it's time to start looking at how to unlock that potential by delving into detail into the main obstacle that everyone faces - the fear of public speaking. The next chapter tells us what modern science shows us about the ancient roots of this fear and shows how this knowledge is the first step to overcoming it.

Chapter 2
Fear of Public Speaking

The Science Behind Your Fear of Public Speaking

> But, public speaking is not just an art - it's also a science.

At the start of the last chapter I talked about the art of public speaking, but public speaking is not just an art - it's also a science. What I mean by that is that scientific studies can tell us lots about how to be a great public speaker. The hints and tips that are derived from scientific research into how to be an effective speaker are mostly covered in the following sections, where we look into what I call the 3 Ps of public speaking. But in this section, I want to just deal with one of the key thing's science can tell us how public speaking works - which is why is it such a universally scary experience for us? Understanding our fear helps us to conquer it.

Human beings are the social animals par excellence. We live in complex groups and our positions within group hierarchies are largely determined by what other people think of us. As such we naturally attach much importance to our reputation. Standing up in front of a large number of people to speak is a high-stakes opportunity to significantly enhance our reputation. When we're up in front of an audience it is an opportunity to prove that we are up for the task and capable of exceeding all expectations.

Psychologists have traced the fear of public speaking right back to the dawn of humanity. Evidence from the fossil record shows that humans were often hunted by other animals who were quicker, stronger or bigger than us. Our response as a species to these threats was to use the one thing that we were undoubtedly the best at - working together.

Humans' big brains allowed us to collaborate in complex ways which protected us and, sometimes, even turned the tables on the animals who were physically better equipped - the hunter became the hunted.

But what's all this got to do with the nerves you feel when standing up in a 21st century office to give a presentation to your colleagues, or when invited to say a few words at the wedding of your best friend? It's because groups were so important to our evolution, that the fear of being thought of badly by a group, and at worst being ostracized altogether, is so acute. Located deep in our brain is the link between rejection by the group and death, and not just any type of death - a lonely and painful one of being forgotten by your peers and abandoned to the mercy of ferocious animals.

Does this all sound too far-fetched? It's just a theory of course, but it would explain the very real results that equate fear of public speaking and fear of death. It's also a helpful theory to bear in mind when dealing with our own fear of public speaking - what we are confronting is not just some weakness in ourselves, it is a universal human fear which is hard-wired into our brains, we should feel comforted to know that everyone, even those who outwardly appear the most confident, still have inside themselves this anxiety; it is part of what makes us human.

And it's not just public speakers who have this fear, it's shared by everyone who performs in public, whether athletes, musicians, singers, and actors.

Fight or flight? What's Happening Inside Our Bodies When We're Afraid of Public Speaking

Stressful situations, like public speaking, trigger the "fight or flight" response in humans. The interaction between your brain, hormones, and the adrenal glands in your kidneys triggers a massive release of adrenaline into your blood. Your blood pressure rises, and your digestive system turns off to make sure that your body can direct its full attention to the organs it needs to deal with the threat. This is great stuff if you're about to start swinging punches or running for your life, not so much if you're just standing on your stage getting ready to address an audience.

It gets worse. What's going on inside you then starts to become outwardly visible. Contraction of the muscles in your back and neck cause you to slouch - almost as if your body is trying to hide itself away in the fetal position. Attempting to resist this natural reaction by pulling your head and shoulders up produces shaking in your hands and legs as your body instinctively readies itself for an imminent attack. Flipping the off switch on your digestive system produces butterflies in the stomach and a dry mouth.

At these moments your body seems to be betraying you, its best efforts to prepare for battling a saber-toothed tiger, are doing exactly what you don't want it to be doing when required to give a talk. Your dry mouth makes it harder to form the words you need and to project them with the confidence you want. Your dilating pupils undermine your short-range eyesight but improve your long-range vision, thus making it harder to read your notes, but easier to spot disapproving faces in your audience.

And science also tells us that we are indeed hard-wired to spot the least happy faces in our audience. A study in 2009 by German psychologist Matthias Wieser found that people who were told that they would have to give a speech had significantly increased sensitivity to pictures of angry faces. Our nerves make us notice disapproving looks and those same looks, tied up as they with ancient fears of ostracization and subsequent attacks by saber-toothed tigers, feed our further nerves.

At this point you might be wondering what's the point of all this science about the fear of public speaking? Maybe it just makes it seem like the fear is an ancient enemy so intrinsic to being human that we cannot hope to defeat it? And a cunning enemy at that, which traps us in negative cycles in which our nerves make it harder to perform, and the worse we perform the more nervous we become. But actually, there are great benefits to understanding the science behind the fear of the public speaking and the ways in which it manifests. Understanding the universality of this fear helps us to recognize it as something natural, which is intrinsic to being human. Knowing that is the first step on the road towards defeating it.

The next three chapters describe in detail exactly how we can use what we know about the science, and the art, of public speaking to transform ourselves from fear-filled early humans to 21st century speaking superstars.

Three key takeaways

1. Fear of public speaking is hard-wired into our evolutionary make-up with roots in the days when group approval was literally a matter of life or gruesome death.
2. So everybody suffers from it, even outwardly super-confident people - it is part of what makes us human.
3. Those unhelpful manifestations of the fear that you feel are also all natural, understanding that can help us to tame them (the next section explains how...)

THE 3 Ps OF PUBLIC SPEAKING
"There are three things to aim at in public speaking: first, to get into your subject, then to get your subject into yourself, and lastly, to get your subject into the heart of your audience." - Alexander Gregg

So far we've looked at the history of public speaking, seen how essential it is to the history of humanity and the significance it's had throughout history and up to the modern day. We've also seen how fear of public speaking also has a history as long as our species, and is also part of what makes us human. Now let's look in detail about what we can learn from the great speeches of history and modern science to see how we can all overcome our fear and bring out the superstar public speaker hiding inside us. I've split this into three sections under the headings of the 3Ps of public speaking, which are:

- Prepare
- Practice
- Present

A successful presentation is always the result of hard work is required at each of these stages. Here's the good news, we can break down each of these stages into simple steps that anyone can follow. Steps which, taken together, become the route to public speaking success. Let's start with our first P – prepare...

Chapter 3

Prepare

Prepare

> Preparation is the essential bedrock on which your success as a presenter is built.

"Fail to prepare, prepare to fail" - it might be an old cliché, but there are reasons why certain phrases become old clichés, and it's normally because they're true. Preparation is the essential bedrock on which your success as a presenter is built. In this chapter we will learn:

- How an ancient Roman politician can help you get your next big presentation ready
- What are the key questions to ask yourself when preparing a talk?
- How to prepare your speech's structure, paying particular attention
- How to choose the words you'll use - taking account of what science tells us about charismatic leadership tactics

How a Roman politician who died over 2,000 years ago can help you get ready for your next big work presentation...

One of the great things about learning public speaking is that we are trying to pick up a skill which everybody struggles with, and a skill which has been demonstrated to us on countless occasions by those experts who overcame their fears to become superlative speakers. Put more poetically we can say that when it comes to developing our public speaking abilities we can "stand on the shoulders of giants", using the learning that we can take from previous greats and using it to our own advantage.

And giants in the field of public speaking don't come much bigger than Marcus Tullius Cicero.

Cicero was a Roman politician and philosopher who is still considered by many the greatest speaker who ever lived even now over 2,000 years after his death. Some speakers may measure their quality in terms of hits on YouTube for their talks. Cicero's is measured by having preserved much of the philosophy of the Ancient Greeks, inspired the entire European Renaissance, and laid the groundwork for modern republics like the United States.

Fortunately, in between all his other achievements, the great man left us some pretty specific instructions about how to deliver a great speech. If you want to speak like Cicero a great place to start is his five-point plan for creating and delivering a great speech. Three of the points relate to how you prepare, and these are:

- **Invent** - work out your key message, your main points and the evidence that backs them up
- **Arrange** - work out the best structure to use for your talk to achieve maximum impact
- **Stylize** - work out the right words to use to present your key points through the structure that you've set
- **Memorize** - committing your speech to memory to ensure you can give it as you planned
- **Deliver** - working out exactly how you will say your speech for maximum impact

The final point (deliver) I'll consider in the next chapter (practice). But let's focus for now just on the first four of Cicero's stages. In order to invent, arrange, stylize, and memorize a great speech its essential to ask yourself the following questions as part of your preparation:

Why are you giving this talk?

The answer to this might simply be "because my boss told me to..." But even if that is the answer it's best to give some further thought to establish the real purpose behind your talk, i.e. what are you ultimately trying to achieve, either on a personal, corporate or even humanitarian level (maybe the purpose of your talk is to raise awareness and inspire action to address a particular issue)?

Knowing the answer to this question is an essential first step that guides all the rest of your presentation. Because, as bestselling author Harvey Diamond put it, "if you don't know what you want to achieve in your speech your audience never will."

You could be asked to speak for any of a million and one specific reasons, but whatever the specific detail the overall aim of the talk will almost certainly fall into one of the following categories, which I call the 5 Es of public speaking purpose - to Entertain, Educate, Encourage, Entice, and Eulogize. Each of these is described in more detail below.

Entertain - this includes talks such as graduation ceremonies, wedding receptions, or awards acceptance speeches. Entertainment speeches are typically light-hearted and joke heavy, bearing significant similarities to stand-up comedy. An example of this type of speech is the tradition of US Presidents giving entertaining speeches at the White House Correspondents' Dinner.

Educate - this includes such types of talks as school and university lectures, informative presentations, product demonstrations or "how to" presentations that share specific skills. These types of talks are heavy on facts and, sometimes, statistics and often make use of presentation slides and visual aids. A purely educative talk is not aiming to bring about any specific change or to sell a particular product or idea, it is purely about the sharing information. An excellent example of an educative talk is Steven Pinker's TED talk, "Is the World Getting Better or Worse? A Look at the Numbers" (spoiler alert - it's getting better).

Encourage - this category includes types of speeches that involve inspiring someone to change their heart or mind to take action based on a particular cause. An example of this type of speech would be an aspiring politician summoning up her own deeply felt emotions and trying to inspire the same feelings from the audience. A classic example of an inspiring speech in this category is Martin Luther King's "I Have a Dream" address in 1964.

Entice - this category is related to the one above in the sense that it is also about encouraging change and action, but the action in question is very specific. This would include advertisements aimed at the purchasing of particular goods or services. Examples of famous sales pitches would be Steve Jobs' launching of new iPods, iPhones, and iPads.

Eulogize - these are the types of speeches which pay tribute to somebody or something, and are often the most emotional type of addresses. This category encompasses things such as the eulogy at a funeral or the speeches given by politicians in response to a tragedy. A famous example of this type of speech is President Reagan's "Address to the Nation on the Explosion of the Space Shuttle Challenger" in 1986.

Of course, these categories are not mutually exclusive. You can, for example, entertain as you educate, and educate as you inspire action, but it is always essential to bear in mind which of the five types is the primary purpose of your speech, and to tailor your words and style accordingly. Building on our earlier example, Steve Jobs' famous launch events to introduce new iPhones were entertaining and informative, however Jobs' primary purpose was clearly to entice people to go and buy Apple's new products.

Working out which category your speech falls into has implications for it in terms of its style and substance, as summarized in the table below.

Purpose of speech	Style	Substance
Entertain	Light-hearted	Full of humor
Educate	Informative	Full of information
Encourage	Inspiring	Full of passion
Entice	Persuasive	Full of solutions
Eulogize	Serious	Full of emotion

What are you going to talk about?

Why you know your overall purpose you can start to think about what specifically you are going to talk about. For Cicero this was all part of the stage called "invent" you've worked out your key message, now you can work out the substance of your talk, brainstorming your key points, and assembling the evidence that backs them up.

It is highly recommended that you make sure that you are an expert in whatever subject you are going to talk on, and if you're required to give a talk on a subject that you don't know that much about then it's essential that you start learning all about it as part of your preparation. This ensures you can select the best information to include and that you will appear highly credible to anyone in the audience who does know a bit about the subject by making sure you cover the major points and don't omit anything crucial or obvious from your presentation.

More than this - many presentation situations also include the possibility of questions after you've spoken. In which context it's a very, very good idea to learn as much as you can about your subject, beyond what's just in your slides, and also to take time thinking about what sort of questions might come up and researching the answers.

Even if your talk doesn't include scope for questions, ensuring you know more about the subject than what is on your slides also helps you to deal with the psychological challenges of public speaking. As the American academic and business guru Michael H. Mescon once said, "the best way to conquer stage fright is to know what you're talking about."

Giving a presentation about a subject you know little about is like skating on thin ice. A single crack, be it from a forgotten line, a curveball question, or a look of disdain from an audience member who knows more than you, can be enough to send the whole presentation crashing down into the icy waters below. Giving a presentation on a subject when you've got a strong base of knowledge about it is like skating on a lake that's frozen solid. Even little cracks don't matter because you can still fly along confidently, safe in the knowledge of the substance that lies beneath your feet.

But working out what you're going to talk about is not just about knowing the subject inside out it's also determined by the answers to the next set of questions…

Who are you going to talk to and where are you going to talk to them?

An essential element of preparation is finding out as much as possible about the audience that you're going to whom you're going to speak. Who are they, what level of knowledge do they already have about the subject, what are likely to be their attitudes, what sort of references and in-jokes will they be familiar with, what can you do to establish a rapport with them? Doing all this allows you to tailor your speech appropriately, taking account of whether you're talking to students or professors, millennials or baby boomers, midwestern Republicans or East Coast Democrats.

Where you are going to talk to them is also important - get to know if you can the venue for your talk, what facilities does it have that you can use, how are the acoustics, will you be speaking with a microphone or not, if it's a historic venue adding in some reference to the history of the place itself can be a nice touch that shows that you've done your homework, especially if what you say will help you to connect with the audience who have gathered there (the venue might indeed be a special place for them too).

Also knowing where you're going to speak helps you to visualize the talk in advance and therefore to perform better on the day (think about the home team advantage in sports - performing in familiar surroundings has scientific benefits. So, if you can take advantage of this by familiarizing yourself with your venue in advance.
The positive psychological effect of all the above preparation is very neatly summed up in a quip from an award-winning Malaysian public speaker, Johan Ooi, "know your venue, know your audience, know your topic, no fear."

When will the presentation finish?

One final detail to consider before we get into the meat of your preparation is the very simple, but sometimes disastrously overlooked, question of how long you have got to speak. It is simply essential to understand the parameters for your talk, especially how long you have been allocated and whether your talk will be followed by a question and answer session. If you don't understand how long you've got to speak you run the risk of the disastrous situation were the MC for the event is having to interrupt you before you've got to the end of your speech.

You must make sure that you take account of the timing in your preparation, and later in you practice - so that you are only preparing the amount of material that will fill the space you've been allocated, and so you can time yourself and verify that you will finish as close to your allocated time as possible.

How are you going to arrange your thoughts?

When you've covered all the steps above you have reached the end of the stage that Cicero called "invention" - you know why you're talking, what you're going to talk about, you've made yourself an expert in your content and you've even done some additional research into your audience, your venue and you fully understand the parameters within which you've been invited to speak - most importantly the time frame you've been allocated.

Now it's time to start getting into the detail of how you're going to get your message across. This is the part of preparation that Cicero called "arrange". Arranging the mass off information that you have at your fingertips about your subject into a winning presentation that achieves your objective may seem a daunting task, but fortunately once again we are standing on the shoulders of giants, and our man Cicero had a six-point plan for arranging his speeches here's his ready-made structure for your speech which has stood the test of over 2,000 years of time.

1. **Introduction** - set out your credentials and get the audience on your side
2. **Narration** - clearly outline the facts that relate to your topic straight away
3. **Division** - explain the opposing schools of thought on the facts, making clear which side you are taking
4. **Proof** - provide the evidence that explains why you take that side and use it to convince your listener of the same
5. **Refutation** - address each of the key points of the other side and explain them away (this is equivalent to the objection handling of a classic sales pitch)
6. **Conclusion** - summarize your key points and end by arousing the emotion of your audience

Another way of thinking about arranging your thoughts comes from the research of Nancy Duerte who studied the greatest speeches of all time to identify the commonalities in the way in which they were structured, What Duerte concluded that the great inspirational speeches focus on problem solving by switching between portraying the world as it is (i.e. setting out the problem that you want to change) and then painting a picture of how it could be (i.e. setting out your solution and what the result would be of implementing that). The speeches Duerte studied often moved back and forth several times between the two worlds, before ending with a powerful vision of the new norm that we could create if we follow the speaker's vision.

Martin Luther King's "I Have A Dream" speech is a powerful example of exactly what Duerte describes. It shifts back and forth between the realities of black American life in the 1960s, and King's vision of what America could be like if only the potential of its democracy was realized through racial justice. Here's just a single sentence that shows the power of the structure of switches used by King, "the whirlwinds of revolt will continue to shake the foundations of our nation until the bright days of justice emerge." Then, of course, the speech finishes with an inspiring evocation of the new norm that King is urging America to create, the harmonious land of which he dreams.

As the above suggests there are different ways to structure talks, what is important is that you do your research and find whatever is best for you taking into account the questions you answered at the start of your preparation for the presentation (what's the purpose of your talk, who are you talking to, etc.). Before moving on from structure though I want to say a bit more about the introduction and conclusion of your speeches. Both because these sections are inevitably common to whichever structure you choose, and because they are undoubtedly the most important parts of your speech. Let's start, naturally enough, with the introduction.

How should you structure your introduction?

Every speech is going to start with an introduction, but what has an introduction got to do? Two things are crucial - to grab the listeners' attention, and to establish your credentials - or phrased slightly differently, to get your audience listening to you and to convince them why they should keep listening to you.

The first point is even more important now than it was in the time of Cicero, after all he didn't have to worry about his audience checking their phones or scrolling through Instagram. If a speaker was in town that was the big event, and Romans generally were keen to lend their ears because they didn't have so much to distract their eyes relative to people in the modern world. Also think about the even greater added importance of your opening in a world where it's entirely possible that the majority of people who will listen to your speech aren't even in the room when you give it. Prominent speeches find a much greater audience online long after their live delivery is done and dusted. Think about famous TED talks, how many people hear them live, a few hundred, a few thousand tops? Then think about how many people watch them on YouTube - as of now (2020) there have been over 18 million views for Sir Ken Robinson's iconic 2006 talk, "Do Schools Kill Creativity?" and the TED Talks series as a whole has received over a billion views.

Why is it even more important to grab your audience's attention (and to hold it) when your videos going to end up living on YouTube? Because YouTube itself is doing its best to distract the viewer with its algorithm induced recommendations on the right hand side of its screen, designed to appeal to that particular viewer and sure to tempt her away if what you're saying fails to grab her and hold her tight (plus you're also competing with the entire rest of the world of the internet into which she could disappear at the single click of a mouse).

The second point, about establishing your credentials, is still as important now as it was in Roman times. People need to know why they should be listening to you and what qualifies you to be talking about the subject. An experiment by psychologist S.F. Paulson in the 1950s showed how much more likely an audience was to change their mind following a presentation when told that the speaker was a "professor" vs the impact had on an audience who received the same presentation from the same person but were told that he was a "student".

Now, of course, I'm not suggesting for one minute here that you should lie about your credentials to achieve your purposes. But what I am saying is that your credentials matter to the audience, and if you do have the credentials to speak on a subject, and you almost certainly do or else why are you giving the talk, then it makes sense to emphasize them and to do that right at the start so you grab their attention and hold it - this person is worth listening to.

There is a rather tricky balance to be struck here between telling people why you're so great and knowledgeable, and between appearing humble so that they like you. Best thing is to drop your credentials in somewhat subtly, don't bash the audience over the head with a sledgehammer as you proclaim how great you are. While it's important to portray yourself confidently a little bit of vulnerability in a speech can be a good way to get the audience on your side, don't be afraid to admit previous mistakes, especially not if you're explaining in your presentation how you're thinking has changed on a topic - taking your listeners on a personal journey with you can also be a great way to help them change the way they think about the subject too.

If you're looking for a fantastic, but highly inaccurate, example of being humble in a speech think about Lincoln in the Gettysburg Address. "The world will little note, nor long remember what we said here", mused the President in the middle of his brief remarks which are still considered, over 150 years later, one of the greatest speeches ever given.

How should you structure your conclusion?

The conclusion of your speech is, of course, your final opportunity to drive home your key points to your audience and to win them over with a last argument or appeal to their emotions. Science shows that it's the part of your speech that is also most likely to be remembered, so you have to make sure it is memorable enough to be captured in the notoriously forgetful human memory.
Here are some suggestions for an effective conclusion structure and some key points to think about when planning your conclusion.

1. Remember the purpose of your talk and plan your conclusion accordingly - remember the first question you asked yourself at the start of this preparation section? Now it's time to revisit your answer to make sure that your conclusion is entirely geared towards achieving the point of your talk.
2. Make it clear that you are coming to your conclusion - it's a good idea to signpost it as it signals to the audience that the key points of the talk are now coming and, even if they haven't been paying that much attention before as long as they listen now they will still get your main message and, hopefully, respond to it
3. Restate your key points - the classic advice when structuring a talk is to tell your audience what you are going to tell them, then tell them it, and then tell them what you told them. The conclusion is the ideal place to restate, briefly, all your key points as it's your last chance to drill them into people's brains, and science shows that lots of repetition is necessary to get messages through and to make them stick
4. Inject emotion - if you're looking to bring about change through your speech then reaching your audience emotionally is key, building that emotion at the end of the talk leaves them with a strong feeling and makes them more likely to respond positively to your call for change

5. Use a story or quotation that powerfully makes your point for you - Human beings are story-telling animals, and our brains are wired to remember stories much better than we do just straight information. If you have a story, either a personal anecdote or otherwise, that clearly illustrates the points you've been making then the conclusion is the place to tell it. In the absence of a story a great quotation can also do the job.

The words we choose for our conclusion are particularly important, and even if we aren't blessed with the gift of composing great poetry or memorable aphorisms, history is full of people who were, so call upon their words, if they're suitable, and use them to your advantage. A well-chosen literary quote also credentializes you further as a cultured person. Make sure, however, to double check any quotes you use to make sure they were genuinely said by the person to whom they're attributed (or risk looking a bit foolish if any audience members know better).

6. Conclude with a call to action - go back once again to the purpose of your speech and conclude with a call to action which is directly related to it. Always remember what you want to achieve and make it clear how people can do it.

Finally, if you'd like a sneaky means to score yourself a much-coveted standing ovation at the end of your speech consider some of the tactics I've seen employed by unscrupulous speakers over the years. Like, for example, making the conclusion of your speech more audience interactive, putting on some music and telling everyone to get to their feet, and then concluding your speech while they're all standing anyway - and there you have it, a guaranteed standing ovation!

What will you say to get your message across?

By the time you've done all of the above preparation you have covered two, out of the five, things that Cicero says are essential for creating a great speech - invent and arrange. That is to say you know what you want to say and the order in which you want to say it. The next step in preparation is working out exactly how you're going to say it or stylize as Cicero put it.

You might think that when you know what you want to say, and you've got the structure of your speech worked out that you're pretty much good to go. After all, don't all the great speakers just look as if they're ad libbing within a rough structure of what they planned to talk about, finding the right words off the top of their heads on the spur of the moment and stringing them together in winning ways?

It might look like that, but the truth is anything but. As Mark Twain famously said, "it usually takes me about three weeks to prepare a good impromptu speech." The much-coveted ability to look like you are just delivering a speech off the cuff only comes with lots of preparation and practice. The latter is the subject of the next section of the book, but here we're talking about preparation and specifically the sort of preparation that features working out exactly what you're going to say down to the detail of the words you plan to use. For Cicero this was the fourth stage of putting together a great speech - when you memorize what you are going to say.

This doesn't necessarily mean that you have to write out every word of your speech, learn it like a film script and then deliver it verbatim (that is an option - but, as I'll show in the next chapter, a less than ideal one). What it does mean is thinking though the key words you want to use to best get your message across, and then using them as the solid base for your speech from which you can improvise should you wish, like a jazz musician knowing an old standard by heart, but then departing from it to meet the needs of the audience and the moment.

Of course I can't tell you exactly what words will be most suitable for your speech, but I can give some science-based hints and tips about the types of things you should bear in mind when putting your words together and when working out what style to use. The suggestions below are largely from the work of John Antonakis from the University of Lausanne (as published in the Harvard Business Review). Antonakis and his colleagues studied the characteristics of charisma and concluded that, contrary to popular belief, charisma is not an innate quality that certain lucky individuals are simply born with, instead it is something that we can learn through the application of what Antonakis called Charismatic Leadership Tactics (or CLTs). Antonakis' research, which focused particularly on the use of charisma in speaking, showed the positive impacts that learning and applying CLTs could have, one group of young executives he studied saw a 60% increase in their ratings as leaders just from building CLTs into their speeches. A few of the most relevant CLTs include:

- Using metaphors and analogies - to communicate complicated concepts in terms that everybody can understand
- Telling stories and anecdotes - to personalize your message and make your audience relate to you
- Asking rhetorical questions - to encourage audience engagement with what you're saying
- Breaking things down into three - part lists - people tend to be able to remember things that come in threes easier (think of the amount of old fairy tales passed down by word-of-mouth which feature the number three)
- Taking a moral stance - to show your character and to encourage your audience to side with you

Does all this preparation sound like a lot of work? It is. I like a quote apparently attributed to a man named Wayne Burgraff which says, "it takes one hour of preparation for each minute of presentation time." But I actually think it's at least double that if you don't know the subject so well and need to fit in all your subject matter research as well as working out your structure and your words.

But all this preparation is well-worth it if you want to be a success in public speaking. Another quote I like, from Management Consultant Somers White, says "90% of how well the talk will go is determined before the speaker steps onto the platform."

The level of preparation described above is a great way to start to overcome all your pubic speaking fears, because the more you prepare the more confident and fluent, you'll be on the day. But all this initial preparation is not, on its own, enough. It's also essential to give lots of time over to the second P of public speaking which is the subject of our next chapter - practice.

Chapter 4
Practice

Practice

The natural place to start practicing is on your own.

Neuroanatomist Dr Jill Bolte Taylor is well-known for her TED talk "My Stroke of Insight" which has had over 6.5 million views on YouTube. Watching it she appears a natural, confident in her material, commanding the stage, and captivating her audience. How many times do you think she practiced the talk before giving it? The answer is 200.

And here's the key thing, you don't get invited to give a TED talk unless you are both a leading expert in your field AND already a great speaker. It's worth repeating that, despite having these two things in her favor, Dr Bolte Taylor still practiced 200 times before delivery. "Practice makes perfect" is an old mantra but it's clear that one of America's leading experts on the functioning of the human brain, agrees...

In fact, everybody who gives advice on good public speaking, from Cicero to Chris Anderson (the Head of TED), always emphasizes the importance of rehearsal. For Cicero this was the final stage of putting together a great speech - working out exactly how you intend to deliver it. The Bolte Taylor example might be an extreme one, but actually it is impossible to over-rehearse, the more you practice the smoother and more comfortable you'll be. As every actor knows the more you've rehearsed the more natural, you'll appear.

In this section I'll show you how to practice overcoming your fears of public speaking and turn the great presentation that you've prepared on paper into a superstar speech.

How to Practice

The natural place to start practicing is on your own. Lots of traditional public speaking advice recommends practicing into the mirror, so you can see how you can across and judge your own body language as well as your words. It might feel a little bit awkward at first, but you can rest assured that lots of great performers, speakers, and singers started out with just the mirror as an audience and used it to hone the skills that they later displayed in front of millions.

There is an alternative school of more modern public speaking thought which proposes breaking the mirror rule. Proponents of this opinion argue that performing into the mirror can cause you to become over-fixated with the detail of your facial expressions which your audience will never see. That may be valid advice but with lots of speeches nowadays either blown up on big screens or broadcast over the internet it is possible that your audience will actually be as close to you as the mirror.

Ultimately, whether you choose to practice in front of the mirror or not is up to you, it's a question of what you feel comfortable with and what works for you. In addition, or as an alternative, to the mirror you may choose to make a video of yourself speaking which you can come back to and analyze. This gives another view of your performance which you can repeatedly analyze to identify strengths and weaknesses and then try again to see how you can improve.

My top tip for practicing is that when you feel a comfortable you present to a trusted friend or colleague whom you can rely on to give honest and helpful feedback. For preparation nothing beats appearing in front of an actual audience, even if it's only one person, their feedback can improve your presentation, boost your confidence and make it easier to face the full audience.

The ideal is to try out in front of your friends or trusted colleagues, take their feedback, and then try again, as many times as possible until you've perfected your speech. Practicing your speech in front of anyone is a way of exposing yourself to your fear of public speaking, and exposure, according to Stanford neuroscientist Philippe Goldin, is "hands down the most successful way to deal with phobias, anxiety disorders, and everyday fears of any sort."

What are the three areas you should focus on when practicing?

During your rehearsals I recommend focusing on four key areas - what you're saying (your words), what you're not saying (your pauses), how you're combining your words and pauses into an overall speech (your delivery), and what the rest of you is saying while your mouth is talking (your body language). Let's look at each of these areas in more detail.

Your words

I've already given in the Prepare chapter lots of advice on how to put your words together to craft a winning speech. The key thing when practicing is to see how those words sound when spoken aloud, and to check with yourself and others that they appear as convincing when said as they did on the paper. Check with the people giving you feedback if your words are as clear and comprehensible astray could be, is there anything they'd recommend changing to communicate more powerfully?

The key thing to remember here is that is an iterative process. If your practice or your friends' feedback makes you realize that part of the speech you prepared just doesn't work, you must go back to the preparation stage and revise that bit. Bounce back and forth between practice and prepare as many times as you need to until you're ready to hit stage three - present.

When rehearsing is it necessary to take a fully written out version of your speech, commit it to memory and recite it verbatim like an actor? I would say no. My advice would be to just write out and memorize the first couple of minutes, this allows you to start very confidently with the exact words that you have committed to memory through practice.

From that point on its important to remember the structure of your speech and the key points to make in each section, but not necessary to have it all remembered word for word. You'll find that after a strong start you'll feel more comfortable ad-libbing a bit as you go on, which frees you up to respond to your audience's reactions. But of course it's up to you if you prefer to try and remember everything, or even just to read the speech directly from paper, which is less than ideal for appearing confident, but which can be appropriate in very formal circumstances where delivering the exact right words is a high priority.

Your pauses

With all the focus on the words of our speech it's easy to forget something almost equally as important - the pauses. Think about it - how does a speaker come across if she just talks non-stop with barely a second to breathe in between sentences - awkward and nervous. Even if what she's saying is brilliant, it's highly likely that the audience will be focusing on how she's saying it and will be judging her presentation a failure irrespective of the content. This is why it's essential to practice speaking much more slowly than is natural when getting ready for a presentation, it might seem odd at first, but you'll soon get used to it and come to appreciate the benefits it brings.

Well-judged pauses don't just make you look more confident, they also serve to emphasize your points for you, letting them sink into your audience before you move in to the next one. It's for all these reasons that Sir Ralph Richardson, one of the giants of British stage and cinema of the 20th century, said "the most precious thing in speech are the pauses."

And it's also why Simon Sinek, another of the top-rated TED talkers, actually recommends starting your presentation with a little bit of silence to avoid the appearance of nerves that comes with talking straight away. Practice walking out on stage, breathing in deeply, leaving silence hanging in the air, and then begin. According to Sinek this simple, silent start "shows the audience you're totally confident and in charge of the situation."

Your delivery - words per minute, rhythm and tone

Of course, there's no point in exuding this silent confidence at the outset if the moment you do begin speaking you start ripping through your speech at around 350 words per minute like a sports commentator describing the Kentucky Derby. The number of English words spoken per minute in regular conversation by the average American is 150. When you're nervous it's natural for this to go up, so counteract that when practicing with a forced effort to speak slower than usual. Watch, for some inspiration, JFK's inaugural address which he delivered at 100 words per minute, far below his own regular conversational average.

During practice you can record yourself and watch back to calculate your own WPM (words per minute). There's no one ideal speaking rate, and of course it varies a lot depending on the words that you are using, but something between 100-150 is comfortable for a presentation. Interestingly some analysis by British company VirtualSpeech of a small selection of top TED talks showed an average of 174 WPM per minute, with a top rate of 201. I would suggest going significantly above 200 is getting too fast (for comparison auctioneers and sports commentators speak at between 250-400 WPM).

Of course, it is essential that you don't get so hung up on your speaking rate that you end up talking in a monotone speed throughout. Differences in speaking speed bring rhythm to your speech and can be very effective ways to grab your audience's attention, show your passion, and drive home your points. A wonderful example of varying speed and rhythm to make your speech more powerful comes from Martin Luther King's "I Have a Dream", he begins by giving information about the historical and current position of African Americans at a very slow rate of 80-90 WPM, letting the significance of each point sink in.

But when King starts, at around 12 minutes in, to share his vision of what America could like, with his repeated use of the phrase "I have a dream", his rate increases dramatically - rising to a peak of 150 WPM. At this faster pace his speech builds to a crescendo with his declaration "let freedom ring" and the crowd responding to his words, his passion, and the urgency with which he communicates them, goes wild. Notice though, that even at his peak, King is only speaking at an average conversational speed. His dramatic effect was achieved by speeding up from his very slow initial rate, which enabled him to enjoy the impact of building to a crescendo whilst maintaining his clarity and control, still allowing his audience to appreciate his every word.

So, to sum up, speech speed is very important, and there is a real danger that nerves will make you go too fast throughout, appear afraid, and be hard to understand. This can be counteracted by a conscious effort to speak slower than seems natural. But there is no one speed that works perfectly for speeches. Practice is the key to getting your pace right, controlling it and allowing you to choose the places at which you change it so you can use variation to command your audience's attention and to emphasize different key points in different ways.

Varying your speed is not the only way in which your delivery can change the way in which your audience receives your speech. A 2015 study by the organization Science for People, which asked volunteers to score hundreds of hours of TED Talks, found that as well as variation in rhythm, speakers who made frequent changes in their volume, pitch, and level of emotion got higher ratings for credibility and charisma. Vocal variety, that study concluded, helps keep the brain engaged and acts against its natural tendency to wander off to thinking about last night's dinner or next year's vacation plans.

Body Language

The third key thing to focus on when practicing is the one thing that most people forget about, but which is, according to most researchers, more important than what you say and how you say it and that's your body language. Or phrased another way - what the rest of you is saying while your lips are speaking your speech.

Why is body language so important? At the start of this book I talked about what human evolution teaches us about the development of speech, but of course body language is even older than speech itself, which explains why our brain is so adapt at reading those non-verbal signals.

Dr Albert Mehrabian of UCLA made a famous study which concluded that only 7% of what we communicate comes through our words, 38% through our tone of voice, and 55% through our body language. Mehrabian qualified his findings by pointing out that they were from a limited experiment focusing specifically on questions of people's emotional responses (whether they liked or disliked what was being said). But nevertheless, his findings, and those of many others, still confirm the overall conclusion - body language speaks louder than words.

How should you take this into account when practicing? First thing is to know what negative and positive body language look like, the table below gives some examples from head to toe:

Body language	Negative	Positive
Eyes	Looking away from audience or scanning whole room without focus	Focusing in on different individuals throughout speech to encourage connection
Face	Lack of variety of expression to match the emotions of your talk - looking down	Varied expressions in line with emotions of your story - smiling more gets higher scores
Stance	Slumped or slouched.	Power pose - shoulders back, feet shoulder width apart
Hands	Static and not moving	Lots of different gestures to emphasize points
Feet	Repetitive swaying from one foot to the other is distracting	Stepping forward to emphasize a particular point

Next pay attention to your body language when practicing, this can be done by watching yourself in the mirror, but even better if you ask your friends watching your rehearsal to think about your body language and provide you specific feedback on it. Another good hint is to video your presentation and watch it back with the sound off so you will be extra focused on all of that crucial non-verbal communication which your audience will also subliminally pick up.

Need some further proof about how important body language is to your audience? Let's look again at the study by Science of People which asked volunteers to rate TED speakers for charisma, credibility, and intelligence. The interesting thing is they asked half the volunteers to watch the talk with the sound switched off, and what did they find? The ratings for charisma, credibility, and intelligence were basically the same regardless of whether the audience could hear the speaker or not. It's clear that what we say silently through our body language speaks volumes.

The same study also drew a couple of other interesting conclusions about body language that should influence the way you move when speaking. Firstly, it found a correlation between the amount of hand gestures a speaker made and how much viewers liked the talk, suggesting that the greater the variety of hand movement the better. Secondly, they also observed that speakers who smile more were rated more highly for intelligence. This should all be considered good news, relax, enjoy yourself, smile, move your hands - you're already well on the way to winning your audience over.

A final thing to consider when practicing, which is often overlooked, is to take account of any props that you will be actually using on stage. Props can just mean something as simple as the desk your laptop will be on or the clicker that you'll use to scroll through slides, or it could include a product that you'll be demonstrating as part of your talk. Try when rehearsing to use the same props as you'll use when speaking.

The more closely you can recreate the actual circumstances of your presentation the more comfortable you'll be when you get up there in terms of how you position yourself on the stage, how you move around, and what you do with your hands. Fluency in terms of all of these little details communicate your confidence and poise to your audience and position you as a convincing, and therefore successful, speaker.

Taking rest when practice is done

Finally, after all that practice remember to make sure to get proper rest the night before your presentation. Good sleep has many benefits, not least helping us to remember things and to perform at our best the next day. You might even want to consider taking exercise the day before the presentation, avoiding heavy foods in the evening, and resisting the temptation to scroll through your phone when going to bed to ensure that you sleep as soundly as possible. Rest and relaxation are the final steps of preparation before the big day to ensure that your speech goes as well as possible.

If you are struggling to sleep rather than stressing over the minute details of your forthcoming presentation the best thing you can do is to focus on positive affirmations. Talking yourself up with assertions that you are going to be a success may feel a little ridiculous, but psychological studies of Olympic athletes, including one led by US Navy Psychologist Marc Taylor, have shown that they really do work. Taking time to convince yourself of your success and to visualize everything going great, is an excellent way to spend your final time in preparation before facing your public speaking fears.

You may also wish at this time to confront your remaining fears head on, considering what it is you're afraid of and trying to identify why you are scared of it. Thinking what's the worst that could happen should provide you with reassurance that actually the whole business is not as serious as you might imagine. Confronting your fears like this, as well as visualizing your success, can be a powerful way to overcome them.

In the next chapter we're going back to where this book started - as you're about to take the stage to deliver your big presentation. Except this time, you've completed your preparation and practice and all you need to bear in mind are the final few tips to help you get conquer your anxieties and present like a professional.

Chapter 5

Present

Present

The moment has come - it's time for you to give your speech.

You've been watching all the other presenters throughout the day and how natural, cool, calm and collected they seemed. You're feeling the exact opposite. As the audience shuffles in anticipation and the events MC gets up to introduce you, your brain is digging up ancestral fears from a million years ago and kicking off your fight or flight mechanism throughout your body. But there's nowhere to run, and instead all that excess adrenalin is turning your face red, your palms sweaty, and your mouth so dry that you fear every word will get stuck in your throat.

Fortunately, if you've followed this book, you'll have done all your preparation and practice, maybe 200 rehearsals, and you'll also know that 90% of your success in your speech comes from all that work you've done before you step on stage. But there's no doubt in the seconds before you start that last 10% can seem the toughest part of all. This is the real deal, live in front of an audience - how do you take that final step up to the plate and transform all your preparation and practice into a presentation that smashes your speech out of the park? This chapter tells you how...

The audience want you to succeed

I'll start with a story about a friend of mine who was asked to deliver a TEDX Talk in his hometown. It was by far his biggest speaking gig to date, but despite that he pretty much failed to follow all the advice in this book. Pressure of work and life got in the way of his preparation and he ended up writing the speech the night before the event. Practice was in the car on the way to the venue.

By the time he was backstage and about to go out nerves were overtaking him to the extent that he was ready for the flight part of fight or flight and was seriously considering making a run for it.

Then one of his fellow presenters who was backstage with him noticed his fear, stopped him from his pacing around, looked him in the eye and said simply, "the people out there are on your side." It changed everything. One sentence was all it talks to change his perspective, so that he no longer imagined himself entering a lion's den, instead he felt as if he was walking out into a room full of friends, all silently urging him to succeed. Against pretty much all the odds, the presentation was a success.

I'm not sharing this story as an example of what to do. In fact, it's almost exactly the opposite of what you should do. But the point of it is this - the frame of mind you put yourself in immediately before you take to the stage is crucial.

Some psychological tricks don't really have any benefit though. I'm thinking of the famous old one about putting yourself at ease by picturing the audience in their underwear. I've never met anyone who admits to doing this in real life and I'm not aware of any serious suggestions that this is a good tactic. But I mention it here just because it always reminds me of a funny moment in the Simpsons, when Homer takes to the stage to nervously deliver a speech, repeating that mantra to himself. For a moment he becomes relaxed as he pictures the audience in their underwear, but then he looks down to notice he's picturing himself in the same state and ends up leaping behind the lectern to take cover before launching into his disastrous address. Psychological tricks are good but, unless they really work for you, silly tactics aren't the best way forward in serious situations.

The examples above are about the attitude you take to an external factor - the audience. Equally important is the attitude you take towards what's going on inside yourself - as the example below illustrates.

Recasting anxiety as excitement

Performance anxiety is, of course, something that afflicts everybody who is going out to perform in high-stakes situations in front of a crowd. Successful TED presenter Simon Sinek was bearing this in mind when he watched the Olympics and learned from the interviews with the athletes how they reframed the anxiety that they were feeling as something positive.

Sinek observed that whenever an athlete was asked by a reporter if they were nervous, they all replied "no, I was excited." By putting a positive spin on the bodily sensations associated with nerves the athletes were coping with those feelings and even turning them to their advantage. Sinek recommends doing the same thing when faced with a nerve-wracking presentation, recast your nerves as excitement he says, and "when you do, it really has a miraculous impact in helping you change your attitude to what you're about to do."

Practical tips - drinking water and taking deep breaths

Top TED speaker coach, Gina Barnett, similarly advises seeing your nervous energy as something positive, and using it to power your presentation. She also gives some very practical tips for what to do immediately before taking to the stage - like starting to drink water 15 minutes before you speak (to avoid dry mouth). Please note scientific advice would be to not drink coffee before you take to the stage, it's known to heighten anxiety, so is best avoided when you're already feeling stressed.

Barnett also recommends taking deep, conscious breaths when you feel that the nerves are overwhelming you. Deep breathing, as advocated by ancient wisdom and modern life coaches, has been shown to counteract the effects of our bodies' fight or flight mechanism, helping to move us towards the more relaxed state sometimes referred to as "rest and digest", in which our heart beat and blood pressure drop. Also remember at this time your positive affirmations, visualize everything going well and tell yourself that you're going to be a success.

Controlling your breathing, being adequately refreshed, and taking a positive view of what's going on inside you and the situation that you're about to walk into are all great ways to keep cool, calm, and collected just before you go on stage. But what do you do next when the announcer calls your name, and it's time to get up and face the audience and the first seven seconds which, according to much of the science, can make or break your presentation?

The first seven seconds - why first impressions really do count

Did you ever see the '90s movie Jerry Maguire? It was a big hit starring Tom Cruise as a high-powered sports agent who has an epiphany, changes her life, and loses his wife (played by Renee Zellweger). He sets out to win her back with a big emotive speech, until she interrupts him with the famous line, "shut up, just shut up…you had me at hello." Well that's how it is with public speaking too - science tells us that more often than not you win over (or lose) your audience right at the very start, in the first seven seconds of your speech.

Remember that study from "Science of People" that I referred to earlier which asked volunteers to watch TED Talks on mute? As part of the same research they also showed some volunteers just the first seven seconds of a speech (with the sound on) and then asked them to score the speaker for intelligence, charisma, and credibility.

These volunteers' scores were then compared to those of others who'd watched the whole speech (with sound). Incredibly the two sets of scores for each speaker were found to be pretty much the same. The people who'd had the advantage of seeing the whole thing came to the same conclusions as the people who'd seen only seven seconds.

It may seem discouraging to think that all your efforts on preparation and practice might come down to just seven seconds of presenting, but let's recast that as a positive. Thanks to all your scrupulous preparation and practice you're sure to get off to a great start, and within seven seconds you will have already won over most of your audience and already be well on your way to your standing ovation at the end.

During the speech

I've said a lot already about how to prepare the content of your speech and how to practice its delivery so that it is communicated with maximum effectiveness. So here I'm just going to talk about what to do when you are performing and unexpected things happen, which cause you to deviate from your planned remarks and your well-practiced delivery. Here are a couple of examples of some tricky situations and some great ways that you can sidestep them when out on stage.

Talking too fast - for all the practicing you've done trying to speak slowly and clearly, there still remains a risk that when faced with the high-stress situation of presenting for real you will end up talking quicker than you'd intended. If you find yourself doing this then make a conscious effort to slow down, or even just stop altogether for a pause and a deep breath before launching back in. Being able to pause and be comfortable in a few seconds of silence communicates confidence to the audience and allows you to calm down and collect yourself.

Technology fails - computer technology can explore distant galaxies, but why does it seem that it can't flick on a slide whenever you've got an important presentation to make? Technological fails afflict us all eventually in these situations, and if it does happen to you the key thing is to have your reaction already prepared so it doesn't knock you from your stride. Search "Steve Jobs High School Memory" on YouTube to see how he dealt with a broken clicker with humor ("they're scrambling backstage right now...) and a funny anecdote to cover technological failure at a Macworld conference in 2007. As you'll know your presentation inside out anyway from your practice, you should always be able to describe the content of your slides (and promise to send them to everyone later) if the worst comes to the worst and you lose them for good.

Spotting negative expressions in the audience - this can threaten to undermine your sense that the audience is on your side and make you lose confidence in yourself and your speech. The key thing to remember here, as we learned in chapter two, is that our brains are hard-wired to pick out the disgruntled faces in the crowd. Knowing this should make it easy for us to ignore them and not take it so personally. We should also remember when we do spot a smiling, nodding, enthusiastic audience member to latch on to that person for a moment, to speak a few sentences directly to them and to benefit from the positive affirmation coming back.

Worse than just a disgruntled face, what if you're confronted with a heckler from the audience? This is pretty unlikely to happen but just in case it does it helps to have a response already prepared so you can quickly deal with the person and move back to your prepared remarks.

I like the reply to a heckler I once heard in a talk given by the British philosopher Alan Watts, "you can have your time in the questions section, madam." - brief, to the point, and polite. No additional engagement with the person encouraged because that risks getting into a debate with a single audience member which could derail all your plans for the rest of your presentation.

A final piece of advice on delivering the presentation - you've done all the hard work preparing so now you can relax into your delivery safe in the knowledge that you couldn't have done more to get ready for it. You'll maximize your chances of everything going well if you can relax and enjoy, feel the energy of the audience willing you to succeed, read their reactions to what you say and respond to them and, most of all, do your best to have fun.

The end

You've done it, you've reached the end of your presentation and there is only one thing left to remember to do. Thanking the audience for their time and attention is the perfect way to round things off and to indicate to them that now is the time to start clapping. When they do and you're receiving their applause make sure to thank them again, their claps are a gift and one that you should acknowledge with good grace. At this point in the proceedings, with everything done and all your hard work having paid off, it should present no problem whatsoever to say goodbye to the audience with your broadest and most heartfelt smile.

Chapter 6

Finding Speaking Opportunities Through Different Media

Finding Speaking Opportunities Through Different Media

> Although the nerves will never fully go away, you'll quickly find that the more often you speak in public the easier it becomes.

Hopefully after having read all of the above you'll be feeling highly motivated to get out there and start presenting yourself. Although the nerves will never fully go away, you'll quickly find that the more often you speak in public the easier it becomes. The good news is there are many public speaking opportunities available to you - ranging from low-stakes situations where you can start small and get good practice with minimal pressure, to high-profile events where you can get significant career building exposure.

A small selection of the different opportunities that exist are detailed below under the headings of the various media that you can use to get public speaking opportunities. I also note some of the considerations to bear in mind when approaching public speaking engagements through each of these routes.

Radio has been a means of reaching a wide range of people with words ever since the first public broadcast in 1906. Many of the great speeches of the early part of the 20th century were designed for and broadcast via radio, including Winston Churchill's legendary rallying cry to the British during WWII "We Shall Fight Them on the Beaches", Gandhi's powerful call for Indian independence through non-violence "Soldier of Peace", and Franklin D. Roosevelt's famous "Fireside Chats" which talked the US through the Depression.

Radio can be a good way to practice your own public speaking abilities in real-life, but relatively low-stress, situations. For example, talk shows on both local and national radio are always looking for people to make contributions. This can give you an opportunity to practice speaking to large numbers of people on topics that you are interested in, from the comfort of your own home, without the stress of literally facing an audience or your speech having implications for your career.

Obviously not all the same considerations apply when thinking about how you will present when speaking on a medium in which people can't see you. Body language is mute on the radio, and visual first impressions no longer matter. But that just makes it all the more important to focus on the details of your words and the way in which you deliver them.

Lots of the same considerations around preparation (as described in chapter three) also apply if you are planning to appear on talk radio. It's especially important to research the host, so you can find out their style and what their views are on the subject that you're going to speak about. This helps you to know what to expect and to anticipate the questions they will ask so you can prepare responses and appear as fluent as possible when challenged.

The enormous spread of television sets across America in the 1950s, was a game-changer for public speaking, as suddenly politicians and other prominent people could reach an audience of millions who could see them as well as hear them. By 1960 88% of American households had TVs (up from just 11% in 1950) and it was in that year that the first televised debates between two presidential candidates took place, pitting Republican Richard Nixon against the young Democrat John F. Kennedy.

A poll taken after the debate famously found that most of those listening on the radio judged Nixon to have won, whilst the majority watching on television thought Kennedy had triumphed. Nixon, recently recovered from illness, looked sweaty and sickly, in contrast to the cool, calm, and collected appearance of Kennedy who had been working on his tan whilst preparing for the debate. Nixon also made the mistake of looking at the reporters sitting at the side of the room instead of talking to the camera, creating an impression that he could not face the public. In contrast, Kennedy confidently addressed his remarks straight to the camera and through it to the watching nation.

Some have argued that the famous poll findings were based on too small a sample but nevertheless many observers, including Kennedy himself, believed that he won the election that night thanks to TV. Nixon himself reflected in the aftermath of electoral defeat, "I should have remembered that a picture paints a thousand words."

The whole story reinforces a message that is also clear from what psychology tells us about judging from appearances - when it comes to public speaking on a visual medium how you present yourself can be just as important as what you say. It also reminds us that when speaking publicly the priority is to address the most important audience, which in Kennedy's case meant ignoring the few reporters in the room and speaking direct to the 74 million Americans watching on TV.

Speaking on television is not just the preserve of presidential candidates of course, but it can be harder to get yourself TV public speaking exposure compared to the radio. It is possible though, and for some careers (like broadcast journalism) developing the skills to speak on TV is essential.

Although getting on television can be difficult, many of the same skills required for appearing on TV can be practiced by taking advantage of the endless opportunities that the proliferation of social media offers us to broadcast ourselves. This includes both pre-recording something to share on the internet or live streaming via websites like Facebook or YouTube.

Unlike radio, and even television, social media has a long-lifespan and is potentially accessible anywhere, anytime at the click of a search engine. So, choose your words, and the way in which you present them, very carefully. Old social media posts have a habit of coming back to embarrass people later in their career so, think carefully and take care that what you say to get spotted now won't be a source of regret later in your career.

The potential public speaking on the internet is not limited to social media. Webinars and webcasting (which is basically broadcasting online) are both used by both large media outlets and private individuals looking for an audience amongst the internet's 4.5 billion users. The history of webcasting is almost as old as the internet itself; one hit from the internet's infancy was a webcast of an office coffee pot at Cambridge University, England, in the early 1990s.

Nowadays you need to be offering something a lot more exciting than a boiling coffee pot to get online attention. But the good news is that the range of webcasts out there gives you plenty of opportunities to find one that can give you presentation and public speaking exposure. If you'd like to practice your public speaking online without high stakes you can even set up your own webcast, taking advantage of one of the many sites that provide the technology for you to broadcast your own talk live.

Despite all the technological innovations of recent decades, the daunting situation that most people think of when imagining public speaking is the old-fashioned conference speech. Almost all of the hints and tips in this book are applicable to conference speaking. TED talks may be out of reach until your career has really taken off, but the network of local TEDX events that take place around the world are more accessible opportunities to give people with something to say a prominent platform. You can also sign up with your local Toastmasters organization which gives both aspiring and experienced public speakers opportunities to hone their skills in a supportive environment.

When looking for a conference to apply to it's necessary to check out when their "call for papers" period is, and to make sure you can provide a compelling paper within their deadline that closely relates to what you know to be the key themes and objectives of the event. Large events that span multiple days at large conference centers will typically provide multiple opportunities for speaking. A good-sized slot to look for to start with is one that's over half an hour, but less than a full hour. Very short speeches can be even more challenging, because of the need to condense your material, but very long ones are also to be avoided early on in your speaking career.

Bear in mind when applying for these conferences that they are normally not looking for you to be marketing your company or produce, They will be interested in your ideas, and so you should use that opportunity to focus on something that you are interested in and passionate about (whilst always ensuring it aligns with the interests of the audience). Your knowledge will enable you to craft a convincing presentation and your enthusiasm for the subject will help to win over your audience.

It's best to make it clear in your application if the topic you've chosen is not something you work on professionally, but to communicate your passion for it. What the conference organizers are looking for is genuine people who can be relied upon to put in the work needed to develop an engaging presentation. Make sure you use the resources available online to see other people's presentations on the same topics, so you can take inspiration from them, but make sure you stay true to your own voice - originality and authenticity will always be appreciated.

In addition to conference speaking, your job may also require you to be involved in other public-speaking situations such as appearing at trade shows on a booth to present your products or demonstrating them in an infomercial. Whilst this book does not deal specifically with the sort of sales techniques commonly used in these presentations the general tips contained here for public speaking are applicable to these sorts of situations too.

Three Key Takeaways

- When thinking about the type of speech you will deliver you also need to consider the medium through which you will deliver it. Most of the tips in this book are applicable across all media but there are some slightly different considerations to bear in mind dependent on whether you're speaking face-to-face, on the radio, on television, or over the internet.
- Traditional media such as radio and television provide opportunities to reach large numbers of people. Speaking opportunities on the radio, in particular, are very accessible, and provide low-stakes opportunities to practice and build confidence.
- The modern world provides a plethora of opportunities to reach people online through social media and webcasting). Again, these opportunities can be easy to access, but remember to choose your words well, even if your initial audience is small, it is likely that people will be able to dig up your words in future - and they may be used against you...

Chapter 7
Conclusion

Conclusion

There are a couple of classic ways to finish a presentation.

There are a couple of classic ways to finish a presentation, one is to recap all your main points and the second is to end with a story, or quote, that encapsulates your main message. In this conclusion I'd like to do both of those things. I start by reemphasizing the key twenty questions to ask yourself at each step of the way when required to give a speech. I have organized these questions into three checklists, one for each of the 3 Ps.

PREPARE

Here are some of the questions to ask yourself and issues to consider when preparing your speech.

Question	Issues to consider
Why are you giving this talk?	Identify your overall purpose (to entertain, educate, entice, encourage change, or eulogize) and your specific aims / targets.
What are you going to talk about?	Bearing the above in mind what will be the subject of your talk? Brainstorm the issues and make sure you have sufficient expertise on all of them.
Who are your audience?	Find out and write down as much as you can about your audience, so you can tailor your presentation to what you know about them.
Where are you giving your talk?	Familiarize yourself as much as possible with the venue in which you'll be speaking to help you plan the details of your talk and visualize delivering it.

How long have you got?	Ensure you're completely clear about exactly how long you have to deliver your talk and what the format is (e.g. will it be followed by questions?)
How will you structure your speech overall?	Look at examples online to help inform your planning about how best to organize the information at your disposal into a presentation that achieves your aims.
How will you structure your introduction?	While bearing in mind the overall purpose of your talk, think about how to grab your audience's attention and also about how to establish your own credentials.
How will you structure your conclusion?	Again, bearing in mind the overall purpose of your talk, think about how best to reiterate your points and end, if appropriate, with a motivational call to action.
What will you say to communicate your message?	Fill in the detail of your structure by working out what you will say in each section - taking account of such tools as the Charismatic Leadership Tactics.

PRACTICE

Here are some of the questions to ask yourself and issues to consider when practicing your speech.

Question	Issues to consider
How do your words sound?	Do the words you have chosen to communicate as clearly and powerfully as possible in order to achieve the aim of your speech?
Are you pacing your speech correctly?	Are you speaking slowly enough (bearing in mind the natural tendency to speak faster when feeling nervous)? Are you varying pace for dramatic effect?
What is your body language saying?	Consider watching a recording of yourself on mute to better judge your body language. Think about posture, eye contact, gestures, and expressions.
How much practice will you do?	Remember it is impossible to over-rehearse, make time to practice on own and also with an audience of friends / trusted colleagues.
How to make sure you are mentally ready?	Practice positive affirmations and make sure you are able to relax the night before your presentation - exercise the day before and get good sleep.

PRESENT

Here are some of the questions to ask yourself and issues to consider when it's time to actually present your speech.

Question	Issues to consider
How best to prepare psychologically?	Remind yourself that the audience is on your side, recast anxiety as excitement, repeat positive affirmations just before and remember to have fun.
How best to prepare physically?	Make sure that you are well-hydrated (drink water not coffee) and take deep breaths to help move your body out of fight or flight mode.
Are you expecting the unexpected?	Think in advance about how you will deal with any unexpected issues - like technological fails or interjections from audience members.
What to watch out for when presenting?	Check yourself to make sure you are not speaking too fast, focus on positive people in the crowd, and judge audience reactions so you can adjust your speech.
What to remember at the very end?	Remember to thank the audience at the end of your speech for the time they've given you and then thank them again for their applause.

Head for the Stars...

On 12th September 1962, President John F. Kennedy gave a speech to a large crowd at Rice Stadium, Houston that helped inspire one of the most unlikely dreams of the 20th century. "We choose to go to the moon," the President told his audience, "and do the other things, not because they are easy, but because they are hard, because that goal will serve to organize and measure the best of our energies and skills, because that challenge is one that we are willing to accept, one we are unwilling to postpone, and one which we intend to win."

Kennedy was speaking about one of the defining achievements of the modern world, taking humanity to the moon. But his words can also be applied to any of the much more personal achievements that each of us can make in our own lives, all of those moments when we translate our hard work and effort into attaining something that we thought beyond our capacity - like public speaking itself.

Public speaking is not something that we do because it's easy, we know it will be hard. As this book has argued, fear of public speaking is something with ancient roots which explains why it is so strong and so universal across the human race. It is, however, a goal worth pursuing because, just as the space race focused American efforts, it requires us to develop and deploy great energies and skills which, as we have seen, can bring enormous benefits to our lives.

All that remains now is for us to proceed with the spirit that Kennedy invoked in the American space pioneers of the '60s - accept the challenge of public speaking, refuse to postpone it, and start with the positive intention that you will be a success.

Written on the walls inside the Kennedy Space Center in Florida is a lovely Latin phrase "per aspera ad astra", which means "through hardship to the stars". It reminds us that our greatest achievements come as a result of hard work. We all know that public speaking is a challenge. I hope this book has shown you how that challenge can be overcome. I also hope that the advice contained in here will help you to enjoy public speaking and to use it as part of your own career's path to the stars. Good luck and have fun!

www.ingramcontent.com/pod-product-compliance
Lightning Source LLC
Chambersburg PA
CBHW051539240526
45465CB00027B/723